SHAKESPEARE'S
THEATRE

Series Editor	David Salariya
Book Editor	Jenny Millington

Author:
Jacqueline Morley studied English at Oxford University. She has taught English and History, and now works as a freelance writer with a special interest in the history of everyday life. She has written historical fiction and nonfiction for children and is the author of *An Egyptian Pyramid* and *A Roman Villa* in this series.

Illustrator:
John James was born in London in 1959. He studied at Eastbourne College of Art and has specialised in historical reconstruction since leaving art school in 1982. He lives in Sussex with his wife and children.

Created, designed and produced by
The Salariya Book Co Ltd, Brighton, UK

First published in 1994
by Simon & Schuster Young Books

Paperback edition published in 1998
by Macdonald Young Books

Macdonald Young Books,
an imprint of Wayland Publishers Limited
61 Western Road
Hove
East Sussex
BN3 1JD

Find Macdonald Young Books on the Internet at:
http://www.myb.co.uk

ISBN 0 7500 2614 6

A catalogue record for this book is available from the British Library.

Printed in Hong Kong by Wing King Tong Ltd.

SHAKESPEARE'S THEATRE

JACQUELINE MORLEY   JOHN JAMES

MACDONALD YOUNG BOOKS

CONTENTS

INTRODUCTION

This book tells the story of a theatre called the Globe. It was built just outside London in 1599, towards the end of the triumphant reign of Queen Elizabeth I. The Globe is especially famous because the plays of the best known playwright in the English language, William Shakespeare, were written for performance there. The idea of creating plays, and theatres to act them in, was a new and exciting one for the Europeans of the late sixteenth century. This book explains why, and tells you what it was like to work in the theatre in Shakespeare's time.

Shakespeare's plays contain some of the greatest poetry in the English language.

Because they were made to suit the Globe stage and please its audience, people today want to know what the Globe was like. This is not a simple question. Nothing of the Globe now remains above the ground. Shortly after it was built, it was totally destroyed (you will find out how in this book). We have no drawings of it, apart from some tiny sketches on maps. Scholars have tried to reconstruct it from scraps of surviving evidence – from law-suits, builders' contracts, theatre goers' descriptions, city regulations, from its foundations which were uncovered during the 1980s, and from the plays themselves. The scenes in this book are based on all this detective work.

THE EARLIEST THEATRES

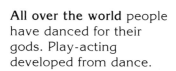

The idea of a theatre – a place where people gather to watch a performance – is very old. Theatres existed in the ancient world, in Europe, India and the Far East. Originally they were not places that provided entertainment. That idea came later. They were temples or holy places where priests or worshippers performed sacred songs and dances, or re-enacted stories of their gods. Both actors and audiences thought of these performances as religious ceremonies.

European theatres began with the Ancient Greeks. Before 500 BC they were putting up open-air seating for watching dancing in honour of the god Dionysus. From about 500 BC they had outdoor theatres with tiers of stone seats, an acting area and a changing room. As part of religious festivals plays were performed in them.

Roman theatres copied the Greek ones, with more elaborate settings. By the time of the Roman Empire (c.27 BC) people wanted entertainment at the theatre, not religion. The Romans' love of stage violence and coarse humour gave the theatres a bad name. The Christians wanted them all closed. They got their wish when the Visigoths sacked Rome in AD 410. There were no public theatres in Europe for the next thousand years.

All over the world people have danced for their gods. Play-acting developed from dance.

Ancient Egyptians (above) dancing with tambourines in honour of the god Bes, in c.1550 BC.

A Chinese theatre (above) c.1500 AD, probably put up for a performance in a temple courtyard or at a public festival.

In the East the theatre kept much closer ties with temple drama than in the West. There was also a tradition of travelling entertainers.

Bugaku (right), a sacred dance, still performed for an audience in Japanese temples. Below, a Bugaku dancer's mask.

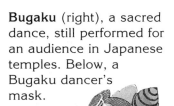

Ancient Greek 'horse' and rider, c.550 BC, part of an animal dance for the god Poseidon.

Indian temple dancers, 10th century AD, in a sacred dance honouring the Hindu god, Krishna.

Native Americans of a Sioux tribe, dancing to summon the great Bear Spirit.

The Lion Dance of the Tutsi people of central Africa is danced to overcome evil spirits.

Ancient Greek theatre (left), c.400 BC. The 'chorus' of dancers exchanged comment with the actors, to unfold the story.

Comedy evolved alongside serious plays, to provide lighter entertainment. Above, Ancient Greek travelling farce-players.

Roman theatre (left) of 55 BC. Seating and acting areas have been united in a big semi-circular building.

The Romans imitated the low comedy that the Greeks acted on their portable stages. Below, Roman comedy figures.

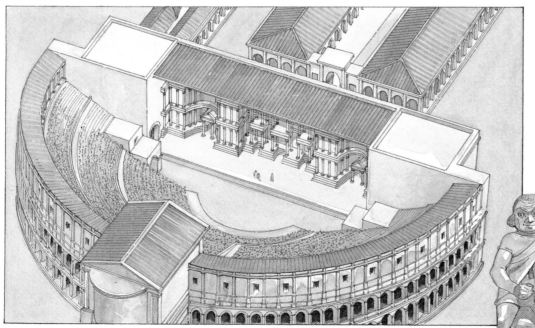

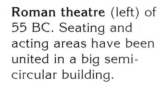

MEDIEVAL THEATRE

In the medieval world there were no buildings that we would call theatres, but that does not mean that there was no acting and no plays. The early Christians had denounced theatres for providing brutal and stupid entertainments that corrupted people's souls. But by the 10th century the Church itself was beginning to discover a use for acting. During the service on Easter Sunday, priests began to emphasise the meaning of the holy day by acting a simple scene of the moment when the angel tells Mary that Christ is risen. Most people could not read, and this was an excellent way of teaching them. Simple scenes celebrating events in the life of Christ were soon introduced on other days of the year. The scenes grew more elaborate, until, by the 14th century, they had become a series of plays telling the Bible story from the Creation to the Resurrection.

The plays drew such crowds and needed so many actors that it became more convenient to stage them outside the church than in. Local people began to take an active part in the staging – contributing money, making costumes and props, and acting parts. The feast of Corpus Christi in June became the day on which the most spectacular series of plays was put on.

10th-century priests enact the Easter story. Here the angel appears at Christ's tomb.

Scene from a 14th-century staging of the Christian story (left). A temporary stage has been set up across the west front of a cathedral. Herod is ordering the killing of the children. To the right, devils wait for him in Hell's mouth. The stage would have several structures on it, representing different places, and the action would move from one to the next.

The Corpus Christi plays (above) lasted all day. Ways of staging them varied. In some countries each play was acted on a wheeled stand, which travelled through the streets, stopping to perform before different audiences. In others, fixed settings were put up in the main square of the town, and the audience moved between them.

Stands grouped in a circle (below). Some were used to seat the audience, and some to represent places featured in the play. The centre was for acting. The scene below is based on a mid 15th-century French example. There is heaven, with a ladder leading to it, and hell. In the centre is the figure of Christ bearing his cross.

PLAYERS

The townspeople who played such an important part in staging the religious plays no doubt enjoyed themselves a lot. But the purpose of the staging was serious. It was an offering to God. The day-long festivities of Corpus Christi were not regarded as entertainment to pass the time. The people who took part were not paid. Professional entertainers, who hoped to be paid for doing something that was not thought of as work at all, were disapproved of in the Middle Ages. Many people thought they were no better than thieves, for they took money for doing something of no value.

Country festivities celebrating the farming seasons – the end of winter, sowing, and harvest time – were marked by traditional dances, often in disguises. From top of page: Maypole dancing; mummers and dancers in animal costume; the 'green man'.

Mayday was a pagan festival the Church could not stamp out. A young girl played the part of queen for the day.

The Church knew that much country fun, like the animal dances, and the wild 'green man' of the mummers' plays, was pagan in origin. This was another reason why people in authority were suspicious of 'playing' and 'players'.

Medieval people did not distinguish between entertainment (which people today expect to pay for) and general merriment, of the sort that anyone could take part in at festive times. They regarded both as 'play', as opposed to work, and they called entertainers 'players'. The Church taught that idleness was a sin, that players were idle and that it was idleness to watch them. But the closing of theatres had not taken away people's appetite for comedy, tricks and tunes. The most lasting effect had been to deprive players of a work-place, so that they had to wander in search of audiences.

Wandering players (below) set crowds laughing with much the same knock-about jokes and comic characters that the Romans had used, and that the Ancient Greeks had enjoyed before them.

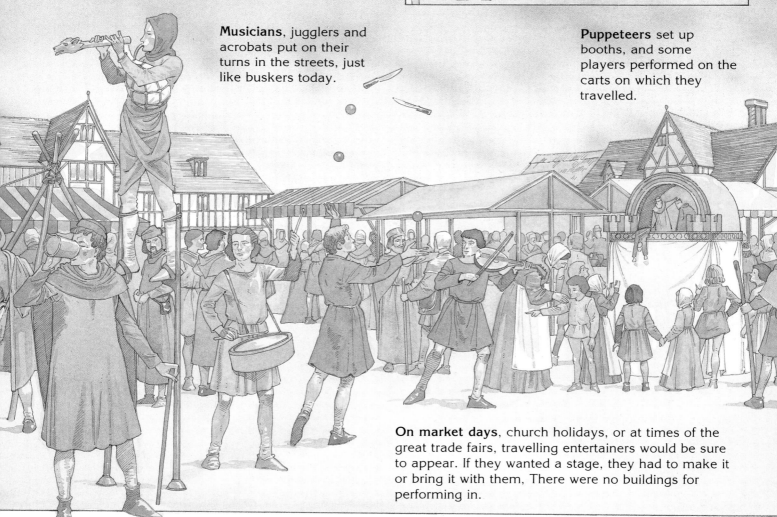

Musicians, jugglers and acrobats put on their turns in the streets, just like buskers today.

Puppeteers set up booths, and some players performed on the carts on which they travelled.

On market days, church holidays, or at times of the great trade fairs, travelling entertainers would be sure to appear. If they wanted a stage, they had to make it or bring it with them, There were no buildings for performing in.

ON THE ROAD

In many parts of Europe during the 15th century wandering players began to form themselves into companies which put together short plays, or 'interludes'. They acted them on makeshift stages in market squares, inn-yards and barns, or any suitable open spot.

These travelling companies were not always welcomed by town officials, who claimed that they encouraged unruly crowds to gather and all sorts of bad behaviour. In 16th-century England they came under particular suspicion. At that time there was a sudden increase in the number of beggars who roamed the country, many made jobless and homeless by recent changes in farming methods. Their plight was not understood, and instead of sympathy they got harsh punishment for being idle. Travelling players risked getting the same treatment unless they could prove they were respectable. The best companies did this by persuading a nobleman to act as patron. He would allow the members of the company to wear his badge and claim to be his 'men', or servants. In return they played for him whenever he wished, and their successes added to his prestige. They got no pay from him and continued to travel for their living. The patron's grand name gave them status, and ensured a better reception.

The players (above) are in luck. They have come to a large manor house. The lord of the manor agrees that they may perform in the hall, for his servants and tenants.

Later (below) they set up their stage in a bear-baiting ring, an open-air enclosure with viewing stands. The players like it, for the audience must pay to get in.

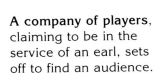

A company of players, claiming to be in the service of an earl, sets off to find an audience.

Their plays are rough and ready affairs, with plenty of songs, jigs and clowning.

In driving rain that soaks their clothes and turns the road to mud they press on to the next village in hope of getting shelter.

On the village green (above) the stage, with its curtained changing booth on top, is soon set up. Money is collected during the performance, but many people try to watch without paying.

An inn-yard (left) is one of the best spots for a play. Inns are busy places, so there is always a good audience. People stand in the yard, and watch from the gallery too.

Wandering beggars are whipped. If convicted twice of being 'masterless' men, they may be hanged.

The players try to keep out of trouble, but two have got drunk and have been put in the stocks.

Now the players have a bad reputation. At the next town they are turned away.

BUILDING THE THEATRE

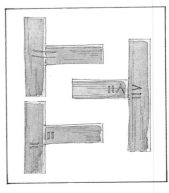

Bear-baiting rings may have suggested the plan of Burbage's theatre. Like them it looked circular, though in fact it had many short sides.

The Theatre's wooden framework was made at the builder's yard.

Then it was taken apart and each piece marked, for re-assembly on site.

The Theatre's stage (right) was like the old travelling stages Burbage had used, except that the changing booth had been enlarged into a two-storey tower. We do not know exactly what Burbage's Theatre looked like, but for reasons that you will find on pages 26–27 it must have been similar in size and shape to Shakespeare's Globe, built 23 years later.

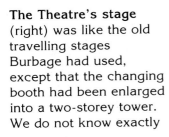

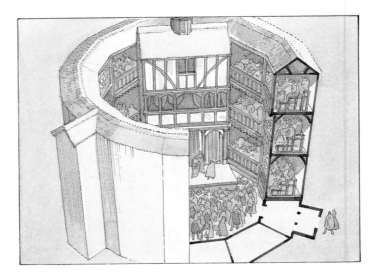

Other people were quick to copy Burbage's idea. Below you can see when and where other theatres went up.

This map is too small to show the many inn-yards that were well known as theatres during this time.

(1) **The Swan**, 1595. A sketch of it survives – the only eye-witness picture of the inside of an Elizabethan theatre.

(2) The Hope, 1614 (also used for bear-baiting).
(3) The Rose, 1587.
(4) The Globe, 1599.

(5) Blackfriars, 1596, used by boy actors until Shakespeare's company took it over in 1608.

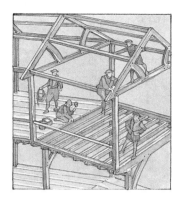

At the site, carpenters matched the marks and set up the frames.

The walls were infilled with interwoven wattle, and plastered over.

Thatchers or tilers covered the roof that sheltered the galleries.

It must have been painted, for it was described as 'gorgeous'.

In 16th-century England most ambitious acting companies went to London to try their luck with the eager city audiences. Playgoing was hugely popular and there were many inn-yards to perform in. The best companies stayed in London as long as they could, although the city authorities tried to restrict the number of performances, and even to ban them, on the grounds that they caused noise and disorder, and lured people from work on weekdays and church on Sundays.

One of the best companies of the 1570s was called the Earl of Leicester's Men. Its manager, James Burbage, was a shrewd and enterprising man.

Burbage saw how people packed the inns to see his company, and knew that he could make far more money by showing plays to bigger audiences. His brother-in-law John Brayne had tried to do so by fitting up a large yard in Stepney. The two men went into partnership and, using Brayne's experience, designed a building especially for staging plays. They leased land just outside London, to the north, where city officials had no authority to interfere, and there they put up England's first purpose-built theatre. The new building was opened in 1576. Burbage named it 'The Theatre'. It was a huge success.

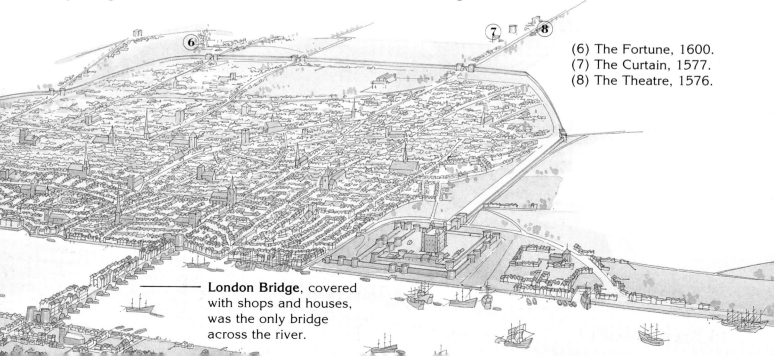

(6) The Fortune, 1600.
(7) The Curtain, 1577.
(8) The Theatre, 1576.

London Bridge, covered with shops and houses, was the only bridge across the river.

HOUSEKEEPERS

Most of the theatres that sprang up in imitation of Burbage's were not owned by actors like him, but by speculators who had built them to make money. A theatre owner was known as a 'housekeeper' because he owned a 'playhouse'. He would let his theatre to a company of players, although not always to the same one, for they were always changing. Players moved from one company to another; companies split up, others joined forces and took another name.

Housekeepers drove a hard bargain. They had money, whereas the players were often poor. A housekeeper usually demanded half the takings. He would lend the company money to buy costumes (a very big expense) and make loans to individual players, for he could always repay himself from the company's half of the takings. We know a good deal about this from an account book that has survived. It belonged to a very prosperous housekeeper, Philip Henslowe, who built the Rose Theatre in 1587 and the Fortune in 1600.

A housekeeper let his theatre to the best company he could get, so that it made him a lot of money. To keep a good company with him, he might make its star players sign bonds promising to pay him a large sum if they left.

The leading company of the 1590s was the Lord Chamberlain's Men (left) who played at the Theatre. James Burbage was an old man by then. Here he is outside his theatre with his sons Cuthbert and Richard, and members of the company. One of the players is William Shakespeare

Star players (right). Here is the famous clown Will Kempe, of the Chamberlain's Men.

Contracts between housekeeper and players were often settled over a meal at an inn. Henslowe paid for the meal when he signed an agreement in 1602 with the Earl of Worcester's Men. Or so they thought – he paid himself back later, from their share of the takings.

Edward Alleyn (below) of the Admiral's Men drew crowds by his powerful performances. Here he is in Christopher Marlowe's play *Tamburlaine*.

Richard Burbage as Richard III. He was a great tragic actor who later was the first to act Othello, Hamlet, and Lear in plays by Shakespeare.

The Admiral's Men (right), at the Rose, were the chief rivals of the Chamberlain's Men. Henslowe is on the right. Alleyn, who was Henslowe's son-in-law and partner, is on the left.

SHARERS AND HIRED MEN

The affairs of a company of players were planned and organised by a small group of its leading members. Each of them provided a sum of money which bought him a share in the company and entitled him to a share in its profits. These members were known as 'sharers'. The Chamberlain's Men had eight sharers in 1596. Among them were Richard Burbage, Will Kempe, and William Shakespeare. The sharers' money went towards the company's day-to-day expenses, which included the cost of costumes, writers' fees, a licensing fee for each new play, travelling expenses while on tour and wages for the hired players.

Bookkeeper

The bookkeeper (left) with the 'scrivener', a person hired to copy out the book, the parts, and the 'plot' – an outline of the play which was pinned up backstage, as a guide for the players.

Scrivener

A company on stage (above) in Shakespeare's *Henry V*. The part of Henry is acted by a leading player. These were usually sharers, who expected to take the big roles. Henry is encouraging his army: players form the front rows, but behind them there may be stage-keepers, and even tiremen or gatherers, wearing helmets and carrying pikes. When a crowd was needed the whole company had to dress up and come on stage.

Stagekeepers

Stagekeepers (above) cleaned the theatre and carried props on stage. Tiremen were responsible for 'attire' (costume). Left, a costume fitting.

Writers were hired to supply plays. Play-going was such a new form of entertainment that there were simply not enough plays to go round. Play writers were known as 'poets', because all serious plays were written in verse. They might be asked to write a new play, to patch up someone else's, or to write one jointly with another poet. It was a job like any other, and not particularly well paid.

Leading players took on boy apprentices (right) and trained them to act. Boys played all the female roles. People at that time believed that acting in a theatre was a most unsuitable thing for women to do, and did not expect to see them on stage. A boy got free board and lodging with his master, who hired him to the company.

Dishonest gatherers had a habit of scratching their heads, in order to drop coins inside their collars.

Hired musicians played sackbuts (like trombones) and drums.

'Hired men', paid weekly, got no share in the profits. Some were players and some were employed backstage. 'Tiremen' cared for the costumes, 'stagekeepers' kept the building in order, 'gatherers' took the audience's money, and a 'bookkeeper' was in charge of the 'book', or text, of the play. He got the necessary licence for it from the office of the Master of the Revels. He had the parts copied out and issued to the players. He noted in his copy which actors were needed, when they came on and off the stage, and what props and sound-effects were wanted. He saw that all this happened on cue.

APPAREL

Costumes and props were known as 'apparel'. They were a company's biggest expense. No cost was spared to make the clothes for important characters as magnificent as possible. Audiences came expecting a brilliant spectacle. They did not expect scenery, for they knew nothing about it – scenery of the kind you would find today in a ballet or a pantomime had not yet been invented. But they were good judges of a lavish display. It was quite usual, in those days, to see processions of magnificently dressed people in London's streets – the lord mayor and his officials, great nobles and their richly decked servants, Queen Elizabeth I and her attendants. On the stage, clothes had to seem just as fine, and this was the responsibility of the tireman.

Housekeepers helped companies to buy clothes, although they expected to get the money back somehow. In six years Henslowe laid out £1,317 on playbooks and apparel – enough to pay six years' wages to fourteen workmen. No wonder that among the fines that a player might have to pay his company – for lateness, drunkenness, etc. – the heaviest of all was for leaving the theatre still dressed in his costume.

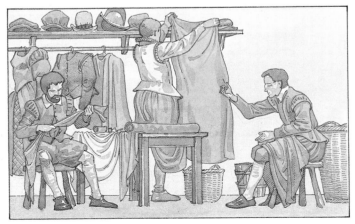

We know little about the tiremen's work, but they probably had a workroom in or near the theatre. It would have been too cramped in the 'tiring room' (changing room) for any but last-minute jobs.

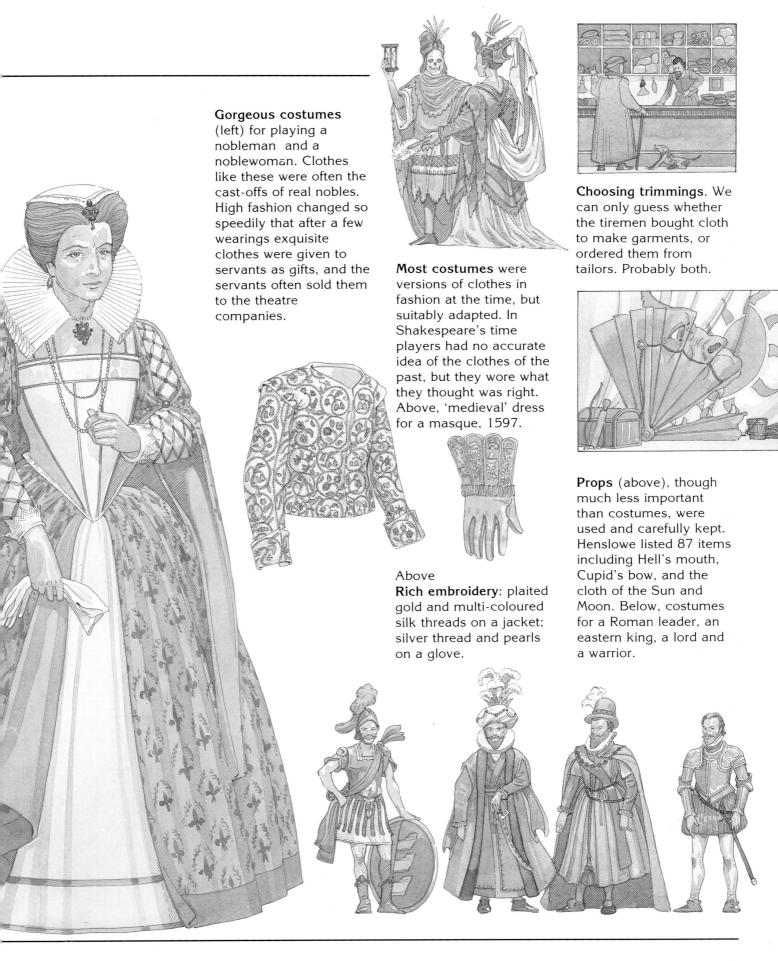

Gorgeous costumes (left) for playing a nobleman and a noblewoman. Clothes like these were often the cast-offs of real nobles. High fashion changed so speedily that after a few wearings exquisite clothes were given to servants as gifts, and the servants often sold them to the theatre companies.

Most costumes were versions of clothes in fashion at the time, but suitably adapted. In Shakespeare's time players had no accurate idea of the clothes of the past, but they wore what they thought was right. Above, 'medieval' dress for a masque, 1597.

Above
Rich embroidery: plaited gold and multi-coloured silk threads on a jacket; silver thread and pearls on a glove.

Choosing trimmings. We can only guess whether the tiremen bought cloth to make garments, or ordered them from tailors. Probably both.

Props (above), though much less important than costumes, were used and carefully kept. Henslowe listed 87 items including Hell's mouth, Cupid's bow, and the cloth of the Sun and Moon. Below, costumes for a Roman leader, an eastern king, a lord and a warrior.

A PLAYER'S DAY

Boys began training from the age of ten or so, acting children and pages till they were tall enough to play women. The best might go on till nineteen, and then become hired men or sharers. Meet Sam, an imaginary player with the Chamberlain's Men, at the Theatre, in 1594.

8 am (left) Sam has been awake since dawn, learning a part. 'Run' yells his master's wife. 'Your master's left. If you're late again you'll pay the fine pay with your pocket money!'

8.15 am (right) Sam rushes into rehearsal and is grabbed by the bookkeeper. 'Ben's got mumps' he says. 'You know his lines, don't you? You'll have to take his part as well as yours. They're not on stage together.'

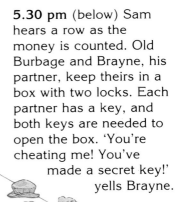

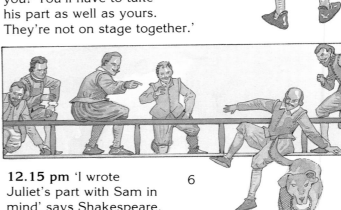

12 noon While munching their pies, the players use the time to consider Shakespeare's new play. He reads it aloud. It sounds promising: good parts, a popular story – *Romeo and Juliet*.

12.15 pm 'I wrote Juliet's part with Sam in mind' says Shakespeare. The men roar with laughter, to Sam's great dismay. But they are not laughing at *him*. The dog has got Shakespeare's pie!

3.30 pm All has gone well. The audience is in a good mood now and Sam was word perfect. In his own part now, the second heroine Silvia, he appears on the gallery, to a serenade.

5.30 pm (below) Sam hears a row as the money is counted. Old Burbage and Brayne, his partner, keep theirs in a box with two locks. Each partner has a key, and both keys are needed to open the box. 'You're cheating me! You've made a secret key!' yells Brayne.

9 am Rehearsing Shakespeare's play *Two Gentlemen of Verona*. Kempe plays Launce, the comical owner of a dreadful dog. Kempe and the performing dog set the whole cast laughing. Shakespeare begs him not to overdo it.

11.30 am The play, an old comedy written by Shakespeare, has to be brushed up in a single morning. No time to go out to eat. The boys are sent to get hot pies and order ale for everyone.

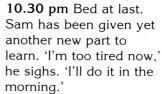

2 pm *Two Gentlemen* is late starting. Some people in the audience begin to stamp and shout. Sam feels anxious as he is dressed for the sick boy's part. He is not sure that he knows it.

2.30 pm The boy playing the lady Julia goes on stage and Sam follows as her maid. As he leaves the tiring room he takes a last look at his part to check what he should say.

10.30 pm Bed at last. Sam has been given yet another new part to learn. 'I'm too tired now,' he sighs. 'I'll do it in the morning.'

6.30 pm Ignoring the quarrel, the cast loads up and sets off to give a private evening performance. Law students want a play in their dining hall. 'They'll be rowdy, after a good dinner,' says Burbage.

ON TOUR

London was the place where players liked to be – no doubt about that. But at times they got out the old carts, loaded them up, and left London for several weeks, or even months, to become travelling players again. They did this most unwillingly, but they had no choice in the matter. Most summers brought an outbreak of the deadly fever known as the plague. People then did not know that rats carried its germs, which flourished in the heat, but they knew that it was passed on rapidly in crowds. As soon as the number of cases suggested a serious outbreak the authorities closed the theatres.

This was bad news for players. Companies cut down the numbers who went on tour, to save expenses, so many hired men lost their jobs. Those that went with the company got lower wages, and none at all if audiences were few and small. They got only rough food, and their lodgings might be an inn loft or a windy barn.

Very often people would turn the players away for fear that they were carrying the plague. When this happened the mayor usually gave the players some money, out of respect for the company's noble patron. In effect, the players were paid to go away.

In bad plague years there was no time for funerals. People laid dead members of their households out in the street each night, to be carted off and buried in pits.

Escaping the plague (above). As the fever spread, Londoners fled to the country. Players' carts joined the queues leaving the city.

Drumming up support (below). The players wanted a good turnout, so they made sure everyone in town knew they had arrived.

A 'mayor's play' (right). If the mayor approved of a company he would pay for the first show, and invite the most respected townsfolk as his guests. This was known as the mayor's play. He might even treat the players to food and ale before they left.

Players acted wherever they could, but they had to get the mayor's consent. Some players, who had been refused at Norwich in 1590, acted in a church. Their manager was put in prison.

Turned out of town (below), some players are asleep under their cart. Another is writing a letter home.

A letter survives from Edward Alleyn, written on tour during the terrible plague of 1593, to his wife in London.

They had only been married a year. The letter is affectionate and touching. You can read part of it on page 45.

A DESPERATE MOVE

At the time of old James Burbage's death in 1597, his family was facing ruin. In 1596 James (enterprising as ever) had spent money converting part of an old friary in London into an indoor theatre. Then local people objected to the disturbance this would cause and he was refused permission to use it. With a useless building on their hands, the Burbage sons also faced the prospect of losing the Theatre. It happened like this: James had built the Theatre on rented land. By agreement with its owner he could use the land for twenty-five years, at the end of which a new agreement had to be made for the Theatre to continue.

In 1597 the time was up, but the landlord would not sign a new agreement. He also claimed that old Burbage had broken promises made in the first agreement and so no longer owned the building he had put on the land. The Burbage sons thought of a plan to outwit this crafty landlord. It was a desperate scheme, but better than losing everything. Secretly, over the Christmas holiday of 1598 when no one was attending to business, they pulled the Theatre down and had its timbers taken across London to the south side of the river. There they used them to build a new theatre, which they named the Globe.

The landlord sued the Burbages afterwards for trespassing on his land to steal the timbers.

We have accounts from witnesses in the case, but we do not know how the dispute was settled.

Breaking up the Theatre was worthwhile because the extra-long timbers needed for its framework were the most expensive part of the building.

The Burbages hired workmen to help them take the building down. It took 3–4 days, time enough for someone to notify the landlord, who was away. He sent an order forbidding demolition, but when his agent tried to enforce it trouble broke out.

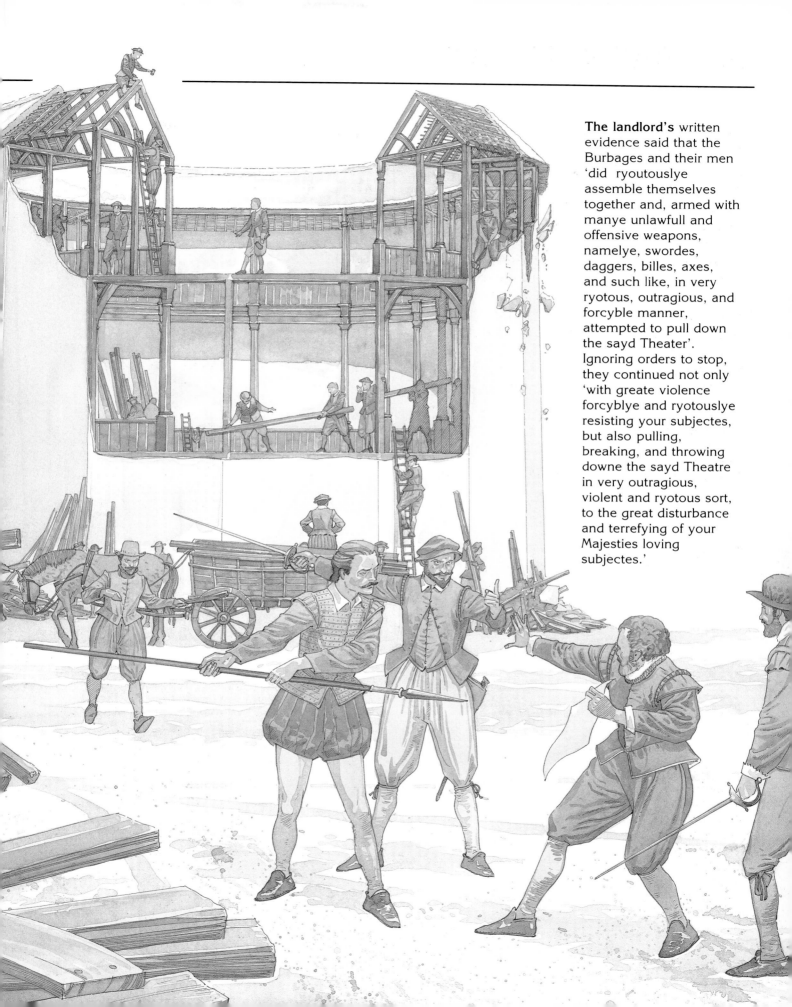

The landlord's written evidence said that the Burbages and their men 'did ryoutouslye assemble themselves together and, armed with manye unlawfull and offensive weapons, namelye, swordes, daggers, billes, axes, and such like, in very ryotous, outragious, and forcyble manner, attempted to pull down the sayd Theater'. Ignoring orders to stop, they continued not only 'with greate violence forcyblye and ryotouslye resisting your subjectes, but also pulling, breaking, and throwing downe the sayd Theatre in very outragious, violent and ryotous sort, to the great disturbance and terrefying of your Majesties loving subjectes.'

THE GLOBE THEATRE

By May 1599 the new theatre was finished. Because it used the framework of the old theatre, which the Burbages had kept up to date by improvements, it cannot have differed greatly from it. Its name, the Globe, made a bold claim. 'There is nothing in the whole round world', it seemed to say, 'which this theatre cannot set before your eyes.' Audiences of the time would have thought this was hardly an exaggeration. The excitement of going to the theatre, then the most thrilling entertainment imaginable, is hard for us to recapture. At the Globe, which ran Shakespeare's two latest plays every year, it must have been electrifying.

How could the Burbages, who were short of money, afford to build such a fine theatre? 'Sharers' were the solution. Re-using the wood saved a lot of the cost. For the rest, the Chamberlain's Men were invited to invest money in the project. Five sharers put up the money, making them joint owners of the building. No other theatre at that time was owned by the players who used it. It gave the company a great advantage, saving the cost of rent and assuring it a permanent home. One of the joint owners was Shakespeare, so this really was *his* theatre.

A performance of Shakespeare's *Julius Caesar* at the Globe (right). From excavations it seems that the Globe was a 20-sided building, about 30 metres across and 3 times as wide as it was high. It held over 2000 people, which means that it was a very large theatre. Ideas about its interior are based on what is known of the Swan (see page 14). People paid a penny to come in (for comparison, a pint of good ale cost two pence). There were two doors, one at the foot of each stair turret, which led, through lobbies, into the yard. People stood in the yard to watch the play. Those who wanted to sit had to pay another penny at the stairs leading to the galleries. A further penny got them a good seat, with cushions.

Southwark, the spot the Burbages chose, was already noted for its theatres, bear-baiting and taverns.

Players came on through two entrances at the back of the stage. The curtain between could be drawn back to show some surprise – a tomb, a laid table, a dead body.

The gallery above the stage was used for balcony or battlement scenes. Musicians played there, and nobles sat there to watch the play.

The stage was sheltered from rain by a ceiling painted to look like the sky. The room in the roof above held machinery which you can see in use on page 30.

BACKSTAGE AT THE GLOBE

The backstage area, between the stage wall and the rear of the building, was known as the 'tiring house'. Here costumes and props were stored and the players got themselves ready. In the early days, tiring houses had been free-standing structures, inside the surrounding frame, but now they were built into the framework. Immediately behind the stage was a packed and jumbled room where everyone and everything needed for the day's play were gathered in readiness. Costumes hung everywhere. Players who had several changes in the play would be dressing or undressing, while tiremen tried to keep the clothes in order. Tables and benches were covered with players' gear: parts to be learned, written out on long narrow rolls of paper; false beards and wigs; and make up – brick dust to redden, flour to whiten, ink for putting on wrinkles.

The play is about to start (below). A player is studying the 'plot'. It is easy to get confused in doing so many plays.

The trumpeter waits for the signal to run aloft and sound his trumpet to quieten the audience before the play begins.

Steps led up to the rooms opening onto the gallery, to the flag turret, and to the room that was right over the stage.

This room held winding gear for lowering a player onto the stage, on a seat disguised as a cloud or a bird, etc,

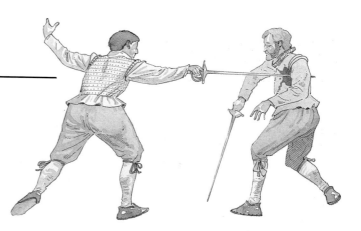

When blood had to flow (above), a vinegar-soaked sponge, under the armpit, was given a hard squeeze. Thunder (right) was provided by drums, or a cannon ball rolled on a metal sheet. Bird song (below) was made by blowing through a pipe into a pot of water.

This is the god Jupiter, descending from the sky, in *Cymbeline*, by Shakespeare. His plays rarely use this effect. It was an old trick, used in the ancient world and in medieval church plays.

A decapitated body (below). The table had a two-piece top, which went round both necks (like the stocks). The side view was hidden, of course.

A trap door in the stage allowed players to descend, as if into a dungeon or a grave.

Ghosts and devils could rise up, swinging sideways as the trap fell, to avoid a bump on the head.

The tiring house also had store-rooms for props and costume. Precious costumes would be kept under lock and key. Another valuable property that would be kept locked away was the store of playbooks. Plays were not expensive to commission but successful ones were very valuable. Companies did not want anyone to print copies.

THE AUDIENCE

Londoners of every sort enjoyed the theatre, except some strait-laced people who thought it wasted time that should have been spent working. The audience – courtiers, merchants, lawyers, craftsmen, idlers and roughs – all went through the doors together. The richer ones sat in the galleries. Those in the yard were a mixed lot: shopkeepers with their families, young apprentices, household servants, soldiers, seamen, fish wives, apple sellers, labourers of all kinds. Women did not go alone, unless they were selling something. Gentlewomen always had a man with them, a servant was enough, to show that they were respectable.

Audiences heckled if they did not like a play. But if they did they listened with rapt attention. Somebody in the gallery once described how the 'sea' of heads in the yard swayed and rippled as every person in it was gripped by the same emotion. We hear of rowdy audiences throwing benches and tiles, and even threatening to rip the theatre to pieces if the players didn't give them the play they wanted, in place of the one on offer. We only know of such things because complaints were made. The normal good behaviour of audiences did not get recorded.

A flag (right) was flown to tell people on the far side of the river that there would be a play that afternoon.

Notices were pasted up (below) to advertise the plays, but there was always the chance that rain would prevent the performance.

Many people (below) came from across the river. There were no tickets or numbered seats so it was wise to set off early. Some went the long way, by London Bridge, but those who could afford it were rowed over in hired ferry boats.

The better seats were nearest the stage, in the sections of the gallery known as 'lords rooms'. The best of all were in the rooms that opened onto the gallery above the stage itself. Vain people liked their fine clothes to be admired in these prominent positions. At indoor theatres (see page 42), fashionable young men sauntered in through the players' entrances and watched from seats on the side of the stage itself.

There were no lights to dim, nor a curtain to lift, to show that the play was about to start. Three trumpet blasts were blown instead.

Impatient folk hurled apples at the stage wall to get the play started.

Refreshments were provided by hawkers of apples, nuts and ale.

'Cutpurse' thieves did well in the crowd, by cutting purse straps.

A MIDSUMMER NIGHT'S DREAM

Today at the Globe the Chamberlain's Men are repeating a popular comedy by Shakespeare. You are in the packed yard. The trumpet sounds and the play begins.

1

3

1. The play opens with a magnificent procession. Theseus king of Athens enters with his bride-to-be. Seated on thrones that have been carried in, the royal pair listen to a request for help.

2. Egeus, a noble, presents Hermia, his disobedient daughter, and Demetrius, his chosen son-in-law. She will not marry him, as she loves another man – Lysander. The king tells her to obey or die.

3. Hermia and Lysander plot to escape through the woods. Jilted Helena, who loves Demetrius in vain, has overheard. She tells the audience her plan. She will betray them to Demetrius, and hope for his gratitude.

4

4. Meanwhile, six craftsmen (the company's clowns) prepare a play to mark the royal wedding. The star is Bottom, the blustering weaver.

5. Night in the wood (but daylight at the Globe). Oberon, the fairy king, meets by chance his queen, Titania. They exchange taunts, for they have had a quarrel.

6. To torment his queen, Oberon sends his servant Puck for a magic flower to rub on her eyes. It will make her love whatever she sees first. Hearing Demetrius spurn Helena, who clings to him as he pursues the lovers, Oberon tells Puck to charm him too.

5

6

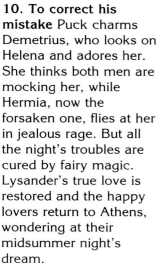

7. Titania sleeps on a bank, under the flower's spell. Puck, seeing the lovers asleep, mistakes Lysander for Demetrius and rubs the flower on his eyes. Lysander is woken by Helena, loves her and forsakes Hermia.

8. Puck plays a trick that will ensure Titania's humiliation. Finding the craftsmen rehearsing in the wood he transforms Bottom's head into a donkey's. Bottom's friends run off in terror at the sight.

9. Titania is awakened by Bottom's singing and braying. Immediately she falls in love with him and begs him to sing for her. She summons her fairy attendants and commands them to lead him to her bower.

10. To correct his mistake Puck charms Demetrius, who looks on Helena and adores her. She thinks both men are mocking her, while Hermia, now the forsaken one, flies at her in jealous rage. But all the night's troubles are cured by fairy magic. Lysander's true love is restored and the happy lovers return to Athens, wondering at their midsummer night's dream.

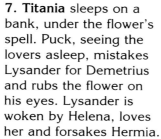

12. The crowds at the Globe applaud loudly, but make no move to go yet. Every play is followed by a jig – a romping dance to send everyone home happy.

11. The play ends in laughter as the craftsmen perform before Theseus and his court. Their play tells the sad story of Pyramus and Thisbe, but its effect is more comical than tragic. The nobles poke good-humoured fun at it.

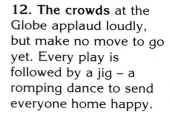

35

THE LIFE OF A POET

Shakespeare was born in Stratford-upon-Avon in 1564. He went to school there, but was not known for his studiousness.

Travelling players (right) often came to Stratford. Young Shakespeare must have been among the children eagerly waiting to see them.

In 1582 Shakespeare married Anne Hathaway, a farmer's daughter. They had two daughters, and a son who died young.

When Shakespeare came to London play writing was still a fairly new craft. Audiences loved violent plays about revenge. They were stirred by poetry too, as the success of Marlowe's plays proved. But plays were not yet valued as literature. If they were printed, their authors were seldom named.

Shakespeare was hired, like any 'poet', to write plays to order. He wrote two a year for Burbage's company, one serious and one a comedy. The people in the yard liked them as much as the lords in the galleries did. Together with Burbage's acting, they made the fortune of the Chamberlain's Men.

From 1600 Shakespeare was at the height of his powers, writing the great tragedies, *Hamlet*, *Othello* and *Macbeth* (below).

Shakespeare was a player as well as a poet. He is said to have taken roles like the ghost of Hamlet's father (left).

He was always very fond of Stratford. In 1597 he bought one of its finest houses, called New Place (above).

By the late 1580s he was in London. How he joined a theatre is not known. Legend says he minded the audience's horses.

Soon he was supplying plays. *Titus Andronicus*, 1591 (above), gave audiences the blood-curdling stuff they loved.

In 1594 Shakespeare joined the Chamberlain's Men and became their permanent poet, working only for them.

Shakespeare was also a good businessman. He was a sharer in Richard Burbage's company when it was still at the Theatre, and amassed enough money to buy a large amount of property in Stratford, and a stake in the ownership of the Globe. It was rare for a player or a 'poet' to become so rich.

Shakespeare had such immediate success that envious 'poets' wrote spiteful things about him, but all the comments we have from those who knew him show how likeable he was. Even in his lifetime he was hailed as a genius and his poetry praised above that of the great English poets, Chaucer and Spenser.

In 1610 he retired to New Place, close to his daughters. He is said to have planted a mulberry tree in the garden.

Business still brought him to London at times. In 1611 his newest play, *The Tempest*, was acted before King James I.

After his death in 1616 two friends collected texts of all his plays, and had them printed in one volume in 1623.

COMMAND PERFORMANCE

According to Ben Jonson, a rival poet, Shakespeare's plays were among those that Queen Elizabeth I liked best. It was the custom at court, during the Christmas holiday, New Year and Shrovetide, for the queen to be entertained with plays. Kings and queens of that period never went to public theatres; the Master of the Revels arranged for the players to come to the Queen at whichever palace she was using at the time. Queen Elizabeth usually wanted to see a new play. The Chamberlain's Men were her favourite company and they performed before her at least thirty-two times. James I was even fonder of entertainments than Elizabeth, and spent far more money on them. When he became king in 1603 he adopted the Chamberlain's Men as his own company and renamed them the King's Men. This made them beyond doubt the leading players. James liked Shakespeare's *The Merchant of Venice* so much that he saw it twice in three days. He and his wife Queen Anne wanted plays so often that there was sometimes a frantic search for something fresh. Burbage once persuaded the queen's officials that she would find the ten-year-old *Love's Labours Lost* as good as new.

It is Christmas, 1594. The Chamberlain's Men have been asked to act 2 plays before the queen. They have rowed down river from London and are arriving at Greenwich Palace. It is quicker and easier to transport their costumes by water than by road.

The great hall of the palace has been turned into a temporary theatre. The queen, sitting in a canopied chair which is a symbol of authority, has an uninterrupted view of the stage. Ambassadors sit beside her. Leading courtiers have seats; the rest stand.

The **Master of the Revels** is responsible for the preparations, which take several days. The palace has to be elaborately decorated. The medieval hall is adapted by putting a platform across its end wall, which has a minstrels' gallery above and two large doorways leading to rooms below. These provide entrances for the players.

Shakespeare is named among those acting before the queen this Christmas but the plays are not. Let us suppose the queen has asked for *Romeo and Juliet*. Shakespeatre might have played the small but important role of Friar Lawrence. Here he enters with a lantern, to find Paris and Romeo dead, and Juliet waking in her tomb.

FIRE AT THE GLOBE

On 29 June, 1613, the King's Men were performing a new Shakespeare play, about Henry VIII. With Burbage in the title role it must have attracted a big audience. We know from a letter written by someone who was there that it was a spectacular production. When Burbage as King Henry arrived at Cardinal Wolsey's house a cannon was fired to announce him. A spark from the explosion settled on the thatch of the roof and set it smouldering, but no one noticed. Those who first smelled smoke paid no heed, and by the time the fire was detected it had got a grip. It must have travelled slowly at first, for, with only two exits to leave by, none of the audience was hurt. One man's breeches caught fire, but with presence of mind he put out the blaze with a bottle of ale.

In less than an hour Shakespeare's Globe was burned to the ground. The King's Men decided at once to rebuild it on the old foundations. By the following summer a second Globe Theatre had opened, by all accounts more splendid than before. Shakespeare was still a part owner, but he had retired to Stratford by now, and this was never his theatre in quite the sense that the old one had been.

Fire smouldering in the thatch could have ringed the whole roof before it became apparent to the people underneath.

The cannon was probably fired from above the stage. Cannon and fireworks were used in lots of plays, in ways that would horrify a modern fire prevention officer.

The theatre, like the majority of London's buildings at that time, was made entirely of timber, lath and plaster, apart from its brick foundations. Once the fire took hold there was no hope of stopping it. There were no fire engines or hoses in those days, only hand pumps, like syringes, that squirted small amounts of water, or buckets in which water from the nearest source was handed along a chain of people.

The new Globe (right). Its exterior is shown quite clearly in a view of London drawn in about 1640. As the new theatre was built on the foundations of the old, the drawing has helped us to form a picture of the old Globe too. It shows a very big building, with two stair turrets and a row of small windows to light the first-floor passage. In the drawing the lowest part is hidden by shrubs.

This time the roof was tiled. The gables over the stage are visible in the drawing, but the interior and doorway are guesswork. More exits must have seemed a good idea!

INDOOR THEATRES

Shakespeare's company, now known as the King's Men, had not only the best players and best plays, it also had the advantage of having two theatres. Old James Burbage (see pages 26/27) had made an indoor theatre in London and then not been allowed to use it. The city authorities wanted to keep players out. In 1595 they forbade the use of inn-yards, but they could not ban the so-called 'private' performances by highly trained schoolboys, coached by their masters. A boys' company had been using Burbage's city theatre, Blackfriars, though their plays were not really private, as anyone could pay to see them.

As boy companies lost favour, Blackfriars fell vacant again. Its owners, the respected King's Men, were able to reclaim it in 1608. The company then spent summers at the Globe and winters indoors at Blackfriars. This was London's first fully professional indoor playhouse, and, like Burbage's pioneering Theatre, its success was soon copied. During the Civil War the Puritans shut all theatres and the Globe was pulled down. After 1660, when theatre designers began work again, people wanted indoor theatres. The Globe seemed a thing of the past. But is this still the case? See page 44.

Blackfriars theatre, as it may have looked. It was much smaller than the Globe, holding perhaps around 800. No one in the audience had to stand. There were benches in the central area, galleries around three sides, probably forming a curve, and boxes overlooking the stage.

The theatre was lit by candles, which had to be trimmed. Pauses while this was done gave rise to intervals.

The King's Men did the same plays here as at the Globe, but as the entry fee was sixpence the audience must have been wealthier.

Above:
Staging a masque (an elaborate danced entertainment) for James I at Whitehall. Several scene changes were made, by sliding painted side panels back and forth in grooves, an idea recently introduced from Italy.

Tricks of perspective were used in painting the panels, to make the audience feel they were looking into an open space. A large rear panel was painted too.

Cutaway view (right) of a later 17th-century theatre – Drury Lane, 1674. It has changeable backcloths instead of a rear wall with doors. Players enter from the sides. A proscenium arch frames the audience's view of the rear stage.

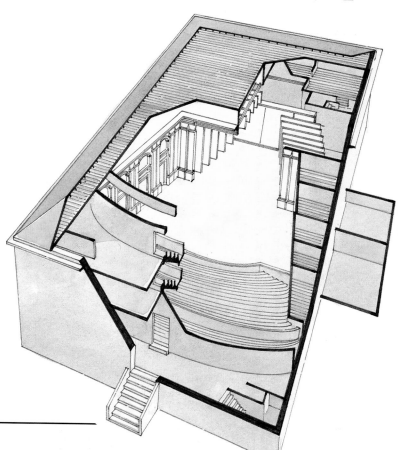

TIME CHART

In all, Shakespeare wrote thirty-seven plays, as well as many poems. This Time Chart only has room to list the best-known ones and those mentioned in this book. The dates of some plays are not known for certain.

1564 Birth of William Shakespeare.

1576 James Burbage opens The Theatre.

1582 Shakespeare marries Anne Hathaway.

1587 The Rose Theatre is built.

*c.***1588** Shakespeare comes to London.

*c.***1590** *Two Gentleman of Verona.*

1592 A serious outbreak of plague closes the theatres for two years.

1593–4 *Richard III, Love's Labours Lost.*

1594–5 *Romeo and Juliet; A Midsummer Night's Dream.* Shakespeare is among players performing for Queen Elizabeth at Christmas.

1595 *Richard II.* The Swan Theatre is built.

1596 James Burbage converts a hall at Blackfriars Priory into a theatre.

1597 Shakespeare buys New Place, Stratford.

1598 *Much Ado About Nothing.* The Theatre is pulled down.

1599 The Globe Theatre opens. *Henry V; Julius Caesar.*

1600 *Hamlet; As You Like It.* The Fortune is built.

1603 Death of Elizabeth I and accession of James I. The Chamberlain's Men become the King's Men.

1603–4 *Othello.*

1606 *Macbeth; Antony and Cleopatra.* First use of painted side wings in a theatre at Ferrara, Italy.

1608 *King Lear.* The King's Men take over Blackfriars as their winter home.

1610–11 *Cymbeline; The Tempest.*

1613 Globe Theatre destroyed by fire.

1614 The second Globe and The Fortune are opened.

1616 Death of Shakespeare.

1619 Death of Richard Burbage.

1644 The Globe is pulled down.

1970 Sam Wanamaker launches a campaign to build a copy of the Globe Theatre on its original site on the Bankside.

1995 Planned first performance at the new Globe Theatre.

A player making his will, in 1605, left several valuable things to his former 'boy': 'I give to Samuel Gilborne my late apprentice, 40 shillings, my mouse-coloured velvet hose and white taffeta doublet, a black taffeta suit, my purple cloak, sword and dagger and my bass viol.' We do not know much about how players treated their apprentices, but it seems from this that Samuel and his master had become friends.

A trickster advertised a spectacular show called *England's Joy* at the Swan Theatre in 1602. It included fireworks, souls in torment, and Queen Elizabeth 'taken up into heaven'. Prices were astronomic – 'two shillings or eighteen pence at least'. The trickster went off with the takings and left a packed house waiting for a play that did not exist. The audience was furious and wrecked the building.

A player called Richard Jones wrote to Edward Alleyn in 1592 asking for the loan of £3 (quite a lot of money) to get his clothes out of pawn, so that he could join a company that was travelling to Germany. English players had a great success abroad. There is an account of people in the Netherlands and Germany following them from town to town, to see them perform again.

Unwelcome visitors in the tiring house: Philip Henslowe noted in his theatre accounts for July 1601 that he been forced to spend six shillings and seven pence for copper wire to mend a tawny coat that the rats had eaten.

Edward Alleyn, on tour on August 1st 1593, writes to his wife in London:

My good sweet Mouse,

I commend me heartily to you and to my father, my mother, my sister Bess, hoping in God though sickness be round about you yet, by His Mercy, it may escape your house...Therefore use this course; keep your house fair and clean, which I know you will, and every evening throw water before your door...and have in your windows good store of rue and herb of grace, and with all the grace of God, which must be obtained by prayers; and so doing, no doubt but the Lord will mercifully defend you....

Now, good mouse, I have no news to send you but this, that we have our health, for which the Lord be praised... I have sent you ...my white waistcoat, because it is a trouble to me to carry it. Receive it with this letter, and lay it up for me till I come...

Mouse, you send me no news of any...such things as happen at home, as how your distilled water proves, or this or that, or anything you will. And, Jug, I pray you let my orange tawny stockings of woollen be dyed a very good black against I come home to wear in the winter.

You send me not word of my garden... remember...that all the bed which was parsley, in the month of September you sow it with spinach, for then is the time. I would do it myself but we shall not come home till Allholland tide. And so, sweet mouse, farewell, and brook our long journey with patience.

GLOSSARY

Apparel, costume, usually in the general meaning of the clothes in a company's stock.

Apprentice, an unpaid trainee craftsman, serving a master craftsman for a fixed number of years, in return for free training.

Attire, costume, usually in the particular meaning of the clothes for a part.

Bass viol, a stringed instrument.

Bearbaiting, the 'sport' of watching dogs fight a chained bear in an arena. Bull-baiting, a similar entertainment, was also popular.

Bond, a written promise that is legally binding.

Book, the text of a play.

Civil War, the war that began in England in 1642 between the supporters of Charles I and those who opposed his policies. It led to the execution of King Charles in 1649 and the establishment of a republican state in Britain, lasting until the restoration of the monarchy in 1660.

Cue, words serving as a signal, in a play, for another actor to speak, a property to be brought on, or a sound effect to happen.

Cutpurse, The sixteenth-century equivalent of a pickpocket. He cut the straps of the hanging purses in which people kept their money. Clothes then did not have sewn-in pockets.

Distilled water, Edward Alleyn is referring, in his letter, to home-made drink.

Farce, a play that relies on ludicrous situations and characters.

Friary, a building, or group of buildings, which housed a community of friars. Friars were members of religious orders. Their buildings had been confiscated by Henry VIII, like those of the monks, which explains why Blackfriars in London was available for conversion.

Gatherer, a person who collected the audience's money at the theatre door.

Green man, a figure in shaggy green costume, sometimes hairy, sometimes leafy, who often appeared in mumming entertainments. He was a survival from pagan fertility customs.

Hawkers, people who go from place to place to sell things.

Herb of grace, the medicinal plant, rue.

Interlude, an early type of play, usually humorous.

Jonson, (Ben), 1572–1637, a famous comic dramatist and writer of poetry, a very learned man and great admirer of Shakespeare's work. Among his best known plays are *Volpone* and *The Alchemist.*

Lath, a thin, narrow length of wood, used to fill in the framework of a timber building.

Licence, a fee paid to the government, for permission to do or to use something. Both Elizabeth I and James I were worried about plays containing speeches that might make people rebellious. Giving or refusing a licence for a play was a way of censoring it, and of getting some tax as well.

Marlowe, (Christopher), 1564–1593, the most outstanding writer of plays at the time when Shakespeare first came to London, and a great influence on him. Marlowe excelled in creating reckless ambitious heroes, in verse of great poetic power. His best known plays include *Tamburlaine*, *Doctor Faustus* and *Edward II*. His career was cut short tragically when he was murdered at a tavern.

Master of the Revels, the official in charge of organising royal entertainments, and licensing plays.

Mayday, an English festival of pagan origins celebrated on May 1st by dances around a maypole decorated with sprigs of greenery, and the crowning of a young girl as May Queen for the day.

Mummers, performers taking part in the traditional medieval custom of dancing and playing in disguises, at certain festivals.

Pike, a weapon with a long wooden shaft and an iron or steel point.

Puritans, people who believed in living a very simple life, based on Biblical teaching. They rejected the authority of bishops who were supported by the king. This was one of the causes of the Civil War.

Proscenium arch, the large central opening in the wall that separates the seating area from the acting area of a theatre, through which the audience sees the stage. It was introduced in Italy in 1619, and became a regular feature of European theatres.

Sackbut, a bass trumpet, with a slide like that of a trombone for altering the pitch.

Shrovetide, the Sunday, Monday and Tuesday before Ash Wednesday. It was a burst of festivity just before Lent. Lent, which begins on Ash Wednesday, is the Christian period of fasting before Easter.

Stagekeeper, a stagehand who was expected to do all sorts of other jobs, from caretaking to playing walk-on roles.

Strait-laced, narrow-mindedly well-behaved and disapproving of others. People of this kind give the impression of being laced into their corsets far too tightly to be able to relax and have a good time. 'Strait' is an old-fashioned word for 'tight' or 'narrow'.

Visigoths, a Germanic people living in the Danube region beyond the borders of the Roman Empire. They invaded the Empire when they were driven westward by the Huns from central Asia in the fourth century AD.

Wattle, laths interwoven with twigs or flexible canes to form a panel.

INDEX

Page numbers in bold refer to
illustrations.

A

Admiral's Men **17**
Alleyn, Edward **17**, 25, 45
apparel 20-21, 42
apprentices 19, **19**, 42
audiences 32-33, **32-33**

B

backstage, at the Globe 30
bear-baiting **14**, 42
beggars 12, 13
Bes 6
Blackfriars (theatre) 14, 42,
    42
bookkeepers **18**, 19
Brayne, John 15, 22
Bugaku 6, **6**
building a theatre 14-15
Burbage, James 15, **16**, **17**,
    22, 26, 40, 42
Burbage's sons (Richard and
    Cuthbert) **16**, 18, 26-27

C

cannon **40**
Chamberlain's Men 18, 22,
    28, 37, 38
Chinese theatre, ancient **6**
Christian plays 9, **9**
Christians 8
comedy 7
Corpus Christi plays 8, 9, **9**,
    10
costumes 20-21, **20-21**, 30
Curtain, The (theatre) 15
cutpurses 33, 42
Cymbeline 31

D

dances, ancient 6-7
Drury Lane (theatre) **43**

E

Earl of Leicester's Men 15
Earl of Worcester's Men 17
Easter plays 8
Egyptians, ancient **6**

F

farming, plays celebrating 10
fire at the Globe 40-41, **40-
    41**
Fortune, The (theatre) 15, 16

G

gallery 33, **33**
gatherers **19**, 42
Globe, The (theatre) 5, 14,
    26, 40-41
    'new' Globe **41**
Greeks, ancient 6
    animal dance of **7**
    theatre of **7**
'green man' 10, **10**, 42

H

Hamlet 36
Hathaway, Anne 36
Henslowe, Philip 16, **17**, 20,
    21, 45
Herod 9
hired men 19
Hope, The (theatre) 14
housekeepers 16-17, 20, 42

I

Indian dances, ancient 7
indoor theatres 42-43, **42-43**
inns 13, 15, 42

J, K

Jonson, Ben 38, 42
Julius Caesar 28

Kempe, Will **16**, 18
King James I 38, 43
King's Men, The 42

L

Lion Dance **7**
London 15, 24
London Bridge 15, 32
Lord Chamberlain's Men **16**
Love's Labours Lost 38

M

Macbeth 36
Marlowe, Christopher 42
masque 43
Master of Revels 19, 38, 39
Mayday 10, 42
mayor's play **25**
Maypole dancing **10**
medieval theatre 8-9
Merchant of Venice, The 38
Middle Ages 10
Midsummer Night's Dream, A
    34-35
mummers **10**
musicians **19**, 29

O, P

Othello 36

pagan plays 10
plague 24
player 45
    day in the life of a 22-23,
    22-23
props 21
puppeteers **11**

Q, R

Queen Elizabeth I 5, 20, **38**

religion 6, 7, 8
religious plays 10
Roman theatres 6, **7**
Romeo and Juliet 22, **39**
Rose, The (theatre) 14, 16,
    17

S

scenery 43, **43**
Shakespeare, William 5, **16**,
    18, 22, 23, 28, 36-37, 40,
    42, 44
sharers 18-19, 28
stage **29**
    building a 14
stagekeepers **18**, 19, 43
stands **9**
Swan, The (theatre) 14, 28

T

Tamburlaine 17
Tempest, The 37
Theatre, The 14-15, **14-15**,
    26-27
theatres, ancient 6
tiring house 30, 31
tireman **18**, 19, 20
Titus Andronicus 37
travelling entertainers 6, **7**,
    11, 36
Two Gentlemen of Verona 23

W

wandering players 11, 12-13,
    12-13
writers 19